Eyespots of a peacock butterfly

The giant spiny stick insect looks like a prickly plant.

Goliath beetle

The termite queen has a very large body.

# Insects and Spiders

Written by Steve Parker

Consultant: Derek Harvey

DK

**Penguin Random House**

**Senior editor** Carrie Love
**Editor** Abhijit Dutta
**US Editors** Margaret Parrish, Allison Singer
**Senior art editor** Ann Cannings
**Art editor** Mohd Zishan
**Illustrators** Abby Cook, Dan Crisp
**Jacket coordinator** Francesca Young
**Jacket designers** Dheeraj Arora, Kanika Kalra
**DTP designers** Dheeraj Singh, Nityanand Kumar

**Picture researcher** Sakshi Saluja
**Producer, pre-production** David Almond
**Producer** Basia Ossowska
**Managing editors** Laura Gilbert, Monica Saigal
**Managing art editor** Diane Peyton Jones
**Deputy managing art editor** Ivy Sengupta
**Delhi team head** Malavika Talukder
**Art director** Helen Senior
**Publishing director** Sarah Larter

**First edition**
**Senior editor** Susan McKeever
**Editor** Jodi Block
**Senior art editor** Jacquie Gulliver
**Art editor** Thomas Keenes
**Production** Catherine Semark
**Photography by** Frank Greenaway
**Educational consultant** John Feltwell

This American Edition, 2019
First American Edition, 1992
Published in the United States by DK Publishing
345 Hudson Street, New York, New York 10014

Copyright © 1992, 2019 Dorling Kindersley Limited
DK, a Division of Penguin Random House LLC
19 20 21 22 23 10 9 8 7 6 5 4 3 2 1
001–31152–Mar/2019

A catalog record for this book
is available from the Library of Congress.
ISBN 978-1-4654-7909-9

DK books are available at special discounts when purchased in bulk for sales promotions, premiums, fund-raising, or educational use.
For details, contact: DK Publishing Special Markets, 345 Hudson Street, New York, New York 10014
SpecialSales@dk.com

Printed and bound in China

The publisher would like to thank the following for their kind permission to reproduce their photographs:
(Key: a-above; b-below/bottom; c-center; f-far; l-left; r-right; t-top)

**8 Dreamstime.com:** Anatol1973 (cr). **9 123RF.com:** Vladimir Jotov (bl). **10 123RF.com:** Brandon Alms / macropixel (bc). **Dorling Kindersley:** Jerry Young (cra). **12 123RF.com:** Agata Gładykowska (b). **13 Dreamstime.com:** Siloto (tr). **14 123RF.com:** Antony Cooper (cl). **15 Depositphotos Inc:** imagebrokermicrostock (clb). **19 Getty Images:** Hans Lang (bl). **20 123RF.com:** Toke Andreasen (tr); Aliaksandr Mazurkevich (bl). **21 Alamy Stock Photo:** Denis Crawford (t). **Dreamstime.com:** Piyapong Singbua (bl). **22 123RF.com:** Gregbrave (cra). **23 Science Photo Library:** Edward Kinsman (bl). **25 123RF.com:** Denis Radovanovic (tl). **27 123RF.com:** Wittaya Puangkingkaew (clb). **29 FLPA:** Edwin Rem / Nature in Stock (cl). **31 123RF.com:** tienduc1103 (br). **34 123RF.com:** alekss (bc). **Dreamstime.com:** Chanwit Pinpart (tr); Mr.smith Chetanachan / Smuaya (bl). **35 123RF.com:** Vadym Zaitsev (tr). **Depositphotos Inc:** okiepony (crb). **37 123RF.com:** bodorka (tl). **Dreamstime.com:** Jacques Vanni (cr). **39 123RF.com:** Francisco de Casa Gonzalez (br). **40 123RF.com:** Chayut Thanaponchoochoung (clb). Gerald Cubitt (br). **42 Depositphotos Inc:** Antrey (c). **Dreamstime.com:** Laszlokupi (bl). **44 Dreamstime.com:** Sergey Khodyrev (bl). **46 Dreamstime.com:** Sandra Standbridge (l). **47 123RF.com:** Kseniya Salostiy (cl). **Depositphotos Inc:** neryx (tr). **48 Alamy Stock Photo:** Martin Shields (cr). **49 123RF.com:** Yaroslav Domnitsky (clb); Vera Kuttelvaserova Stuchelova (br). **50 Alamy Stock Photo:** Denis Crawford (cr). **51 Dreamstime.com:** Marcin Wojciechowski (bl). **53 123RF.com:** Anton Lopatin (crb). **Alamy Stock Photo:** Biosphoto (bl); imageBROKER (tc); Nic Hamilton (cla). **Depositphotos Inc:** Gucio_55 (cra). **54 Dreamstime.com:** Aetmeister (crb). **FLPA:** Piotr Naskrecki / Minden Pictures (cl). **54-55 123RF.com:** Chaturong Gatenil (b). **55 Alamy Stock Photo:** Papilio (br). **FLPA:** Michael & amp, Patricia Fogden / Minden Pictures (tr). **57 123RF.com:** Gefufna (crb). **58 Science Photo Library:** Melvyn Yeo (cr). **59 Alamy Stock Photo:** Nature Picture Library (br). **Depositphotos Inc:** smspsy (tr). **61 123RF.com:** Marco Uliana (crb)

Cover images: **Front: 123RF.com:** Brandon Alms / macropixel crb, Marco Uliana cb; **Dorling Kindersley:** Jerry Young tc/ (Ladybird), cra; **Dreamstime.com:** Alslutsky tc; **Back: Dorling Kindersley:** Jerry Young c; **Spine: Dorling Kindersley:** Jerry Young cb, bc

All other images © Dorling Kindersley
For further information see: www.dkimages.com

A WORLD OF IDEAS:
**SEE ALL THERE IS TO KNOW**

www.dk.com

# Contents

# Looking at insects

Many insects are so small that you cannot see them in detail, so they might not seem interesting. However, with a few pieces of equipment and some practice, you can soon learn about their fascinating ways and habits. Look for insects on leaves and flowers, under stones and logs, and in the soil.

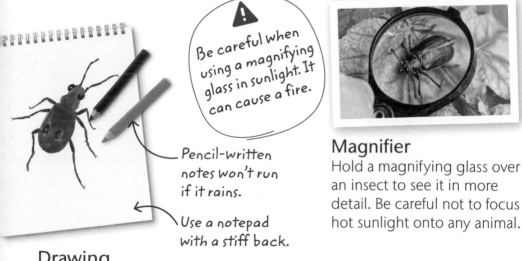

⚠ Be careful when using a magnifying glass in sunlight. It can cause a fire.

Pencil-written notes won't run if it rains.

Use a notepad with a stiff back.

## Magnifier
Hold a magnifying glass over an insect to see it in more detail. Be careful not to focus hot sunlight onto any animal.

## Drawing
Make a sketch of what you see. Label features such as wings or unusually shaped legs. Note the insect's size, color, and where it lives. You can finish the sketch later—and you'll soon improve with practice.

The common tiger beetle, with its bright green color, is easy to spot.

# INSECT PARADISE

An insect hotel provides shelter and protection for your local creepy-crawlies. Attract insects with natural materials stuffed inside plant pots. Line up or stack the pots together to make a multistory hotel.

Dried lavender and seed heads make a perfect place to attract insects. After filling an empty plant pot with these, turn it on its side.

Rolled up cardboard and straw are ideal for insects seeking shelter. Add these to a plant pot.

Gather sticks and dried leaves. Fill a plant pot with these items to welcome creepy-crawlies.

Bees like to live in small holes, like those in bamboo sticks. With an adult's help, cut the sticks so that they fit inside a plant pot.

## Storage jar

A clean glass jar with air holes in the lid makes a good temporary insect home. Always put the insects back outside as soon as you can.

Move and lift small insects on a paintbrush, to keep from squashing them.

# What is an insect?

There are more than a million types of insect. Check that a creature is an insect by using the 3 + 3 rule. A typical insect has three parts to its body: head, thorax (middle part), and abdomen (end part). An insect also has three pairs of legs. Many insects have wings and antennae, or "feelers," on the head.

## Ladybug
This small, tough creature is a type of beetle. Under its hard body covering are two wings that help the ladybug to fly away if need be.

## Butterfly
The butterfly is a fairly large and delicate insect. Butterflies have antennae that they use to feel and smell.

*A butterfly has four large wings.*

## Housefly
Like most insects, the housefly has wings and antennae. It has compound eyes, made up of thousands of six-sided lenses.

*A fly's feet are about 10,000 times more sensitive than a human tongue.*

*It has small antennae on its head.*

*It tastes with its feet.*

*Its wings are attached to the thorax. They flap 200 times a second, making a buzzing sound!*

# Insect in close-up

The common wasp shows all the main parts of an insect. It has four wings, although many insects have just two. The front and back wings on each side are linked together by hooks, so they flap as one. Wasps have bright yellow and black markings to warn other animals that they can sting.

Feelers

An insect's head has two big eyes, feelers, and mouthparts for biting.

The legs have tiny claws at the end for gripping on plants.

An insect's leg has joints that bend as it walks and runs.

The middle part, the thorax, has wings and legs on the outside, and large muscles inside.

Tubes called veins stiffen the see-through wings.

The end part, the abdomen, contains the guts for digesting food, and the reproductive parts for breeding.

Wasps have a powerful sting, so try not to annoy them!

# Are spiders insects?

Spiders are not insects, because spiders have four pairs of legs. A spider's body has only two parts: the first part is a combined head and thorax, and the second part is the abdomen. Spiders are related to scorpions, ticks, and mites. Together, these form the group called arachnids.

Most spiders have four pairs of eyes. These are simple eyes.

Spiders have eight jointed legs—four on each side.

The hairs on its legs act like ears, picking up tiny movements in the air.

The head and the thorax are joined together.

Spiders don't have bones. They have cuticle instead.

The silk-producing glands are present in the abdomen.

## Making silk

Unlike most insects, spiders can make silk. They use it to form egg cases. Many also make sticky webs of silk to catch their food. They wrap trapped insects in it and eat them later.

## MAKE A SPIDER'S WEB

You will need: 13 ft (4 m) flat elastic braid, washer or keyring, wooden board 20 in (50 cm) square covered in colored paper, 12 pushpins, 33 ft (10 m) fine elastic, scissors, tape, and thread.

1. Pull the braid through the washer. Pin the braid in place onto the board.

2. Make another pair of spokes using the braid and pins.

3. Work on alternate sides until you have made 12 spokes.

Ensure the braid is tight.

Trim the ends of the braid.

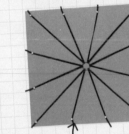

4. Starting at the center, make a spiral with the elastic.

Wind it around each spoke in turn and keep it taut.

When you have finished, ask an adult to pin down the elastic.

# Legs and leaping

Most adult insects move swiftly on their six legs. They may not seem very fast to us because they are so small. If an ant were as big as a human, however, it could run five times faster than an Olympic sprinter, while a human-sized flea could leap over a 40-story building.

The cricket's "ear" lies just below the knee joint.

## Leg joints
Like all insects, this bush cricket has six jointed legs, with stiff straight sections between the joints. It also has special "ears" on its front legs for hearing sounds made by other bush crickets.

The cricket looks around to make sure it is safe to jump.

## Look before you leap
Insects with very long legs, such as crickets, grasshoppers, and fleas, are usually good leapers. The cricket folds its long legs back on each other when it gets ready to leap.

Before it leaps, this speckled bush cricket makes sure its feet have a good, firm grip on the branch.

## Into the air
Powerful muscles in the legs straighten the "hip" joints and the "knee" joints, so that the whole leg is straight. The parts of the leg work like long levers, to fling the cricket into the air. Your arm straightens in the same way when you throw a ball.

Hip joint

Knee joint

Spine

The cricket opens its speckled wings, ready to flutter a short distance, and then glide to land in a safe place.

The cricket can kick out with its spiny legs to defend itself.

## Singing insects
A grasshopper chirps by rubbing its back leg along a stiff vein in the front wing. The leg has small teeth on it, like a comb, which buzz and vibrate. It sings to attract mates and warn rivals.

## Expert digger
The mole cricket's back legs are powerful for pushing through soil. It also has short, wide front legs. These work like shovels to help it dig tunnels in the soil.

# Walking on water

Where air and water meet, a stretchy "skin" forms at the water's surface. Since many insects are tiny, this skin is strong enough to support them. Some bugs and beetles can run on it. Underwater insects hang from it and poke their breathing tubes up into the air, or collect air bubbles.

## Water boatman
Look out for water boatmen, which have long legs that they use like oars to swim in ponds. Some kinds swim upside down on their backs. They hunt tiny fish, tadpoles, and insects. Don't touch—they can give a painful nip.

## Surface skater
The pond skater, a water bug, skims over the water's surface. Its front legs detect ripples from struggling prey and its middle legs help push it across the surface. Waterproof hairs on its feet make dimples in the water as it chases insects.

Rear legs are used to steer.

The whirligig beetle has two pairs of eyes, for seeing above and below the surface.

## Whirligigs
These small, black beetles swim in groups, spinning on the water's surface. They eat dead creatures that fall into the pond and some live ones, too!

# MAKE AN INSECT AQUARIUM

1. A glass fish tank makes a good insect aquarium, but any large bowl will do. Put gravel and small stones on the bottom. Use pond, fresh, or rainwater for your tank. Tap water can contain chlorine, which kills insects. Pour in the water and add the plants until it's about halfway full.

Change two jam jars full of tank water for pond water each day to keep the water fresh and provide food.

Many pond insects can fly. Keep a lid with a close-weave net or mesh on the tank.

Molting insects such as mayflies need plants or sticks above the surface, to crawl up.

Pondweed is food, and insects cling to it and hide in it.

Bottom dwellers such as caddis fly larvae like to hide under stones.

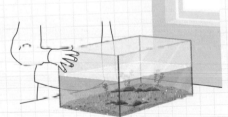

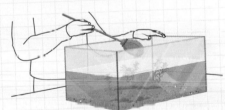

2. Keep the tank in a well lit but cool corner of the room. The water will get too hot in bright sunlight.

3. Tiny plants called algae may grow as a green "scum" on the sides of the tank. Rub them off with a sponge tied to a stick, and filter them out of the water with a strainer.

# On the wing

Most insects have wings and can fly at some stage in their lives. Insect wings are thin and light, and are stiffened by a network of tubes called veins. Strong muscles in the middle section of the insect provide the power for flapping.

## Lacy wings
The lacewing's beautiful pattern of veins in its four wings looks like finely woven lace. This insect flies mainly at night.

## Beetle takeoff
Beetles have four wings. The front pair are hard and tough. They cover the beetle's back and protect the long, folded, flying wings underneath. This cardinal beetle is preparing for takeoff.

*It unfolds and spreads out its main pair of flying wings.*

*The cardinal beetle lifts its red protective wing covers.*

## Up and away
The long see-through wings, with their strengthening veins, move so fast that they become a blur. The beetle flies off to look for more food.

The beetle beats its wings faster and faster until they reach flying speed.

The hard wing cases do not flap at all. The beetle holds them clear of the main flying wings.

## Speeding up
With each beat, the main wings push air downward. This lifts the cardinal beetle upward. Then the wings also begin to push air backward, so that the beetle moves forward. Pushing with its legs against the flower, it springs away. In a flash, the beetle is airborne.

The beetle straightens its legs and holds them down, away from the fast-moving wings.

## Expert flier
Hoverflies are expert fliers. They can hover above flowers, then dart off and reappear a short distance away. They can move in any direction, including backward.

# Feeding time

Some insects can eat almost anything. Cockroaches have strong chewing mouthparts to eat stale food, dirt, and even paper and leather. Other insects have specially shaped mouths. Bugs have a hollow, needle-shaped beak, to pierce and suck sap from plants and blood from animals.

## Nipping weevil

Weevils are a type of beetle. They have a long curved "snout" called a rostrum, with tiny jaws at the end. They bite small pieces of leaves and other plant parts.

## Spearing prey

This diving beetle larva has large, pointed "fangs" for spearing prey. It squirts special juices into the tadpole that dissolve its body into soup. The beetle larva then sucks up the mushy meal.

The curved "fang" is called a mandible.

The long, tube-shaped mouth is called a proboscis.

## Built-in straw

Butterflies and moths have mouths shaped like drinking straws. When they are not feeding, the straw is coiled up. To suck sweet nectar from flowers, it is uncoiled into a straight tube.

This is a hummingbird hawk-moth—it feeds like a hummingbird.

## Ant attack

Ants have strong jaws, called mandibles, which bite and cut up food and enemies. This bulldog ant has especially big mandibles. They seize and chop up other insects for food.

Each mandible moves at a hinge joint where it joins the head.

Spikes along the inner edge of the mandibles give it extra grip.

⚠ Don't touch—bulldog ants can bite!

The ant's mouth is just underneath the base of the mandibles.

## Juicy meal

Spiders have tiny mouths, so they cannot chew their prey. They inject digestive juices into their victims, as this lynx spider is doing, to dissolve the soft parts. They then suck up the juicy mixture.

# Insect-eye view

What does an insect see? Most insects have eyes made of many separate sections, called ommatidia (*om-a-tid-ee-a*). Each section sees a small part of the surroundings. The whole view may look like a patchwork.

*A cicada has three simple eyes.*

*The dragonfly's huge compound eyes take up most of its head.*

## Simple eyes

Besides two main eyes (compound eyes), many insects also have several smaller eyes. These are known as simple eyes or ocelli (*o-sell-ee*), and they do not have separate sections. They probably just detect blurs of light or dark.

*The dragonfly can see in front, below, and behind, all at the same time.*

## All-around vision

It's not easy to get close to a dragonfly, because it can see all around it at the same time. Imagine being able to see behind yourself without turning your neck! Dragonflies hunt by sight.

Each ommatidium has a transparent top to let in light.

Inside each ommatidium, light is focused onto nerves that send signals to the brain.

## What big eyes...

Dragonflies have the biggest eyes of any insect. This helps them to spot tiny flying insects, which they catch on the wing. This is a close-up view of the common darter dragonfly. Each eye has up to 5,000 ommatidia! Many insects can tell colors apart, and many, such as moths, can see clearly at night.

The eyes look for danger, mates, rivals, and places to lay eggs.

## Seeing the invisible

Many insects can detect ultraviolet light. This is light from the sun that we cannot see (but it gives us a tan). Guide lines on petals only show up in ultraviolet light. Honey bees see them and follow them to the nectar.

# Touch and feeling

A good sense of touch helps insects to detect air movements when flying, and to cling onto leaves and stems. Insects feel for footholds when crawling, for food when feeding, and for holes and cracks when hiding.

*Antennae detect scents, tastes, and currents of air.*

## Branching out

Insect antennae are very sensitive to touch. The chafer beetle has branched, fan-shaped antennae. Normally it keeps them closed. When it takes off, the beetle fans out the antennae. This makes it more sensitive to wind currents and any smells in the air.

*Just sitting on a leaf, the chafer beetle keeps its antennae closed.*

*When in flight, it fans out its antennae.*

## Extra-long antennae

The long-horned moth's thin antennae are over twice as long as its body. They bend and wave using even thinner muscles inside them. Big groups of moths dance around trees on sunny days.

24

## Hairy sensors

The long legs of a spider, like those of this Mexican red-knee tarantula, are covered with sensitive hairs. These hairs can pick up tiny vibrations made by insects and help the spider hunt.

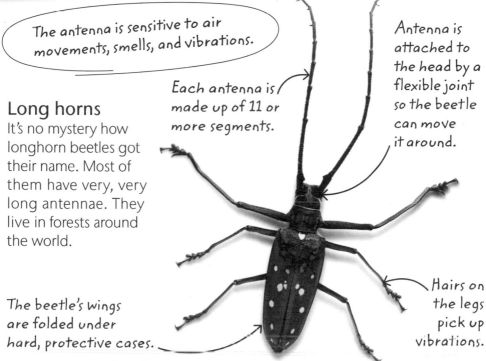

The antenna is sensitive to air movements, smells, and vibrations.

Each antenna is made up of 11 or more segments.

Antenna is attached to the head by a flexible joint so the beetle can move it around.

## Long horns

It's no mystery how longhorn beetles got their name. Most of them have very, very long antennae. They live in forests around the world.

The beetle's wings are folded under hard, protective cases.

Hairs on the legs pick up vibrations.

## Cave dweller

The cave cricket needs long antennae because it lives in dark caves. The cricket feels its way by "tap-tapping" with its antennae—just as you would use a stick to find your way with your eyes closed.

# Taste and smell

Insects do not have a nose for smelling and a tongue for tasting, like we do. Instead, they have tiny taste buds on many parts of the body, mainly on their mouthparts and antennae, and also on their feet! The main parts for detecting smells floating in the air are the antennae.

The bluebottle is a common sight in kitchens.

## Fussy flies

Tasting and smelling usually help an insect to find either food or a mate. This bluebottle fly smells the syrup, which could be food. It lands and checks by tasting, to see if it is good to eat.

The fly spreads digestive juices on the food, which is like vomiting over it!

A fly has taste buds on its feet. These are the first parts to touch the food.

The fly dabs up dissolved food with its spongelike mouthparts.

# TESTING TASTES AND SMELLS

Test which insects are attracted to each dish by smell. When they land and taste it, do they stay or fly off? Do you think they can detect pure water? Wash your hands after this activity.

1. Pour syrup or sugary water into one small dish, a bit of old meat or gravy into another, and tap water into the third.

2. On a sunny summer day, put the dishes outside on a table, 24–32 in (60–80cm) apart. Note which insects visit them in your notebook.

3. Butterflies and wasps smell the syrup, which they eat as food. Flies smell the meat and come to lay eggs, since their maggots eat flesh. No insects smell the water.

## Smelly meal

Look out for dung flies buzzing around dung. They are attracted by the smell of fresh animal droppings! They lay their eggs in dung. When the maggots hatch they eat the droppings, which contain lots of nourishment.

## Follow the smell

When a searching ant finds plentiful food, it lays a trail of invisible scent on the ground, leading back to the nest. The other ants follow the trail and so find the food easily.

# Laying eggs

Each kind of insect finds the best place to lay its eggs. In the wrong place, the eggs could dry out, get too wet, become moldy, or be eaten. Also, the young insects need food nearby when they hatch. A dungfly lays eggs in fresh droppings, because this is what the maggots eat when they hatch!

## Drilling deep

All female insects lay their eggs through a tube called the ovipositor. In some insects, such as this ichneumon (*ik-new-men*) wasp, the ovipositor is like a long needle. It drills deep under the wood's surface, and the eggs slip out of its tip.

The wood wasp taps and prods the wood with her ovipositor, feeling for the best place to drill.

## Eggs in a purse

To protect her eggs from danger, the cockroach lays them into a bag or purse, called an ootheca. She produces this smooth, tough purse from her abdomen.

*The leathery bag contains two rows of eggs.*

*She lays batches of at least 30 eggs on the leaf's underside, hidden from most egg-eaters.*

## Life underneath a leaf

The shiny yellow eggs of a cinnabar moth can be found on the underside of a ragwort or groundsel leaf. The females lay eggs there because the caterpillars (developing moths) eat the leaves when they hatch. This is called laying eggs on the food plant.

*The male damselfly holds onto the female while she lays her eggs underwater.*

## Underwater eggs

Insects such as damselflies and dragonflies lay their eggs in or near water, because the young live in water after hatching. The female damselfly pushes her thin abdomen under the surface and glues her eggs to the plant stems below.

# Changing shape

The worm-like stage of the beetle's life is called a larva.

Many newly hatched insects look different when they become adults. Young flies, beetles, butterflies, bees, ants, and wasps all look a bit like worms. They grow bigger, change their body shape completely, and turn into adults. This is called complete metamorphosis.

As the larva grows, it splits its skin and wriggles out.

### The larva

A newly hatched larva of a flour beetle is a real insect, but it looks like a small worm. It is called a mealworm because it eats "meal," an old name for ground grains and flours, like oatmeal.

New, bigger skin forms underneath. Changing skins like this is called molting.

Chrysalis hangs off a twig.

### Becoming a butterfly

Butterfly eggs hatch into larvae called caterpillars. Each outgrows its skin and becomes a pupa—called a chrysalis (*kris-a-lis*). These hang from branches or on the undersides of leaves. Many look brown and wrinkled, like old leaves. Inside its case the caterpillar changes shape. In a few weeks it becomes a butterfly.

## The pupa

The larva continues to eat, grow, and molt its skin. After about five molts, it turns into the next stage of its life, a hard-cased pupa. The pupa hardly moves at all, but inside, the larva is changing enormously.

Mouthparts

Antenna

Claws on feet

— Pupa

— Inside the pupa, parts of the larva's body break down, then rebuild into a beetle.

## The adult

After a few weeks, the pupa's case splits open and an adult flour beetle crawls out. Only now does it look like a typical insect, with six legs and wings.

Wings are under the wing case on the back.

## Wings out to dry

When an adult insect like this cicada comes out of the pupa, its wings are crumpled. The adult pumps blood into them. The wings spread out, and go stiff and hard as they dry. Then the adult can fly away.

# Growing up gradually

Some insects don't go through as many stages in growth as others. The young of these insects hatch from their eggs looking like tiny adults, called nymphs. These nymphs molt their outer skins many times, changing body size slightly at each molt. This is called incomplete metamorphosis. Insects that grow like this include locusts and dragonflies.

*After the first molt.*

*After the second molt.*

## Hatching
The female locust lays her eggs in a strong case in the sand. The baby locusts hatch from the eggs and dig their way out.

## Getting bigger
Every few weeks, the locust nymph molts and then grows before the new skin hardens. It does this four times. It only has small wings and cannot fly. However, at the fifth molt, an adult emerges from the skin, complete with full-length wings.

*The nymph's claws hold it firmly on the twig.*

*Adult's body enlarges as it pulls its long legs out from inside the old nymph legs.*

*Adult begins to wriggle out of the old skin.*

## Not quite adult

A mayfly nymph lives for years in water, breathing with three tail-like gills. At last, it crawls up a plant stem and splits its skin. However, it's not an adult yet. First, it molts into a subadult, which can't fly very well. The subadult flutters to a bush or tree near the water. In a few hours it sheds a thin skin and becomes the real adult, which can fly much better.

The old skin is now almost empty.

Adult hangs onto nymph skin . . .

## First flight

As soon as its wings have dried, the adult locust can fly away.

. . . as it pulls the rest of its body free.

The adult's wings begin to spread out as blood pumps into their veins.

# Harmful insects

Most insects are not harmful. However, a few cause problems. Some caterpillars, beetles, and weevils spoil crops and damage trees. Cockroaches infest food supplies. Termites weaken wooden furniture and buildings. Some insects kill people by biting and spreading diseases.

## Tropical forest
Different kinds of mosquitoes spread the germs that cause malaria and yellow fever. These illnesses affect warm tropical places such as swamps and tropical forests, where mosquitoes live and breed.

Abdomen full of blood

## Spreading germs
When a mosquito bites a person and sucks their blood, it also takes with it that person's germs. It transfers these germs to the next person that it bites, which spreads diseases. This is more likely to happen in the tropics.

## Beware of the sting
Insects such as bees and wasps have a sharp sting at the rear end. A bee can use its sting only once, but wasps can use theirs several times.

The hornet, a big wasp, can give a very painful sting—so be careful!

The sting pokes out of the rear end as the hornet attacks.

## Potato pest

Colorado beetles love to eat potato leaves. If they breed well, they cause enormous damage to potato crops. Originally, these beetles came from the Rocky Mountains in Colorado, which explains their name.

Aphids tend to probe for sap on the softest parts of the plant—such as new leaves and buds.

## The gardener's enemy

Lots of little insects crawl around on flowers. These are aphids—also called greenflies and blackflies. They use their spearlike mouths to pierce plants and drink the sap. Aphids breed very fast. When the young hatch, they feed on the leaves and soon the plant shrivels and dies. Aphids feed on roses, beans, cabbages, and other plants.

## A deadly bite

The black widow spider is one of the most venomous spiders in the world. Its venom is 15 times stronger than a rattlesnake's. The female is more dangerous than the male.

# Hunting insects

Insects that hunt other creatures need to have large eyes to see their prey, strong limbs to hold it, and powerful jaws to crunch and chew it. Some have stings to poison and paralyze their victims. The hunter on this page is called a praying mantis. It munches on other insects, such as flies—and also on other mantises.

## How to catch a fly
The mantis keeps perfectly still as it watches a fly. Its green color makes it look like a harmless green leaf. Even its eyes are green!

Grasping front legs
have hooks and spines.

The fly explores the
young leaf for food.

The mantis slowly leans forward,
holding firmly onto the twig with
its two rear pairs of legs.

In a flash, the mantis unfolds and
shoots forward its front legs.
It grasps the fly in a strong grip.

The fly cannot
escape from the
spikes on the legs.

## Assassin bug

The assassin bug hides in a flower. When a victim comes near, the assassin grabs it and jabs its long, tubelike mouth into the body. Venom flows down the tube, dissolving the victim's insides, which the assassin sucks up—like you sucking a milkshake through a straw.

## Fly feast

The mantis leans back onto its perch to eat the fly. Its powerful jaws soon cut through the fly's body casing and begin to scoop out the soft flesh from inside.

*Strong mouthparts cut up and devour the fly.*

*The mantis's large eyes keep watch for danger, as well as seeing the best way to eat the fly.*

## A fast runner

Many spiders catch their prey without using webs. The wolf spider uses speed to catch its prey. It runs over the soil and up small plants, catching anything that comes its way.

*The mantis will leave the less nourishing wings and legs.*

# Parasites

A parasite is an animal (or plant) that lives on or in another, which is known as the host. The parasite harms the host, usually by stealing its blood or other nourishment. Several kinds of insects are parasites. Lice, mosquitoes, and fleas suck blood. Many sorts of wasps are parasites on the eggs, larvae, or adults of other insects.

## Weevil hunter

The weevil-hunting wasp chooses big weevils as hosts for its larvae. The wasp grasps and stings the weevil. The sting paralyzes the weevil so it cannot move—but it does not die.

The wasp holds the weevil in position with its strong legs.

The sting enters where the weevil's body casing is thin, usually at a joint.

## Leaping bloodsucker

Worm-shaped flea larvae live in dirt and soil. They turn into adults that pierce the skin of their host and suck the blood. Different types of fleas have different hosts. Fleas from cats, dogs, and rats may bite people.

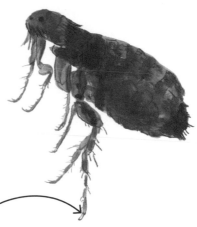

A flea can leap more than 12 in (30 cm) with its strong rear legs.

The weevil can't move.

## Food for the young

Unlike most true parasites, the larvae of this wasp ends up killing and completely eating the weevils. The wasp takes several weevils to her nest, in a burrow she has dug in soil. She lays her eggs on the weevils and fills in the burrow. When the larvae hatch, they eat the live hosts.

Weevils in burrow wait to be eaten.

## Irritating itch

If a flea bites you, it leaves a red spot on your skin that will itch for a few days. Rat fleas spread diseases such as the "Black Death," which once killed millions of people.

# Living in groups

Some insects are never seen alone. These are called social insects—they need to live in a group to survive. Termites are social insects that look and live like ants. They make huge nests, with one queen ruling many workers. Some feed on fungus.

## Egg machine

The queen termite's body is huge. Over time, it becomes bigger to hold more eggs. She mates with the smaller king, then lays 30,000 eggs each day! She is fed, cleaned, and looked after by workers. Soldier termites with strong biting jaws defend her and the nest.

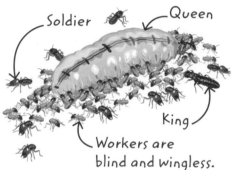

Soldier

Queen

King

Workers are blind and wingless.

## Mending nests

Many animals, including birds, feed on termites. When they try to break into the nest, workers gather to repair the hole.

## A new life

In a big termite colony, some young grow up with eyes and wings. In suitable weather, they fly away to find a mate and start a new nest.

## Inside the nest mound

Some termites make their nests underground, or in trees or old logs. Others construct huge mounds with walls of dirt mixed with termite spit. The air inside must be cool and moist, or the thin-skinned termites will dry out and die.

The hot air escapes up the main chimney.

The termites' hollow nest-cooling chimney may stand 13 ft (4 m) tall. That's the same height as two tall adult humans!

The walls are made of baked, hardened soil and mud.

A cooling breeze of air flows through the chambers.

The queen, king, and royal helpers are deep in the nest's center.

Chopped-up bits of wood and other food are stored in underground chambers.

The main nest is below ground level. It is dark, moist, and cool.

Fungi (molds) may help to rot down the wood, making it easier for termites to digest.

41

# Ant society

Scurrying ants are social insects, like termites. The queen ant is the only one that lays eggs. The workers look after her and feed her. They go in search of food—from plants and seeds to other insects. Certain types of ants have big-jawed soldiers who defend the underground nest.

## Tap tap

Ants pass on information about food, enemies, nest damage, and other matters in two ways. They make special chemicals called pheromones (*fer-o-mones*), which other ants smell. And they tap each other with their antennae.

*If you see ants touching antennae like this, you'll know they're "talking."*

*When at risk, many ants spray a stinging acid chemical from the rear end.*

*An ant can run very fast because of its long legs.*

## Cutting leaves

Ants gather bits of food from plants, small creatures, and rotting material. Leaf-cutter ants snip out pieces of leaves, take them to the nest, grow a special fungus on them, and eat the fungus.

# MAKE AN ANT FARM

Borrow ants from nature and watch them for a few days to see them working together, making a nest, and gathering food. Use an empty aquarium tank, old goldfish bowl, or other ant-tight container.

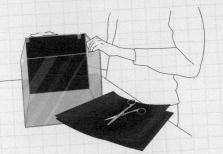

1. Stick dark paper around part of the outer side of the tank. The ants like their tunnels to be dark, so they are more likely to make them up against the dark sides.

2. Look for an ants' nest outside. Under a stone is a good place. Gather a few scoopfuls of ants and soil. Try to get a mixture of different-sized ants.

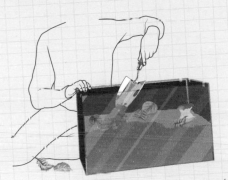

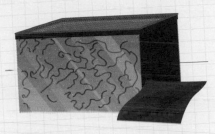

3. Put the ants and soil in the tank. Add more damp (not wet) soil, a few new and old leaves, and a bit of fruit. Make sure air can get in, but ants can't get out.

4. After a few days, gently lift the dark paper. You may see ant tunnels built up against the glass. Put the ants back where you found them after a week or two. The colony won't last long without a queen.

The bee sucks nectar with its tube-shaped mouthparts.

# Busy bees

You may have seen honeybees buzzing from flower to flower. This means that they're collecting food to bring back to their nest or hive (a house built for them by people). Like termites and ants, honeybees live in groups.

## Beeline
When a worker bee finds some flowers that have lots of sweet nectar to collect, it flies back to the hive and "dances" to tell the other workers where it is. Then they fly hundreds of times between flowers and hive.

It carries the food back to the hive.

⚠️ Bees can sting! Watch their antics from a safe distance.

## Bags of pollen
As the bee sips nectar it rubs against pollen grains (yellow powder on flowers). The pollen gets caught on the bee's body. The bee carries the pollen back to the hive in hairy "shopping bags" on its back legs.

## Keeping bees

People keep honeybees so that they can collect their sweet, sticky honey. The bees change the nectar into honey, which they store in honey cells. The beekeeper removes some combs and takes the honey.

## Inside the hive

A big hive may have more than 50,000 bees. The queen lays all the eggs. All the worker bees are female. They feed and clean the queen bee, clean the hive, sting enemies, and look after the eggs and the larvae in their cells. There are also males (called drones) who do not sting. Several drones mate with the queen.

Workers make six-sided cells from wax, which comes from glands under their abdomens.

A worker dances by waggling her abdomen, to tell other bees where the nectar is.

Some cells will contain stored honey, while others will hold eggs and growing larvae.

# Don't touch!

Brightly colored insects in the park or woods are meant as a warning. The bright reds, yellows, and oranges, mostly patterned as spots or stripes, are warning colors. They warn predators such as birds and lizards that the insect tastes horrible, that it bites or stings, or that it squirts foul-smelling fluid.

### Blister bearer

The blister beetle's shiny body warns that this beast tastes bad. If its blood gets on the skin of a person or animal it causes painful blisters. Animals soon learn to leave the beetles alone.

*Blister beetles gather on flowers to feed and lay eggs.*

### I taste horrible

Bright red spots on the black body of the red-and-black froghopper mean it tastes horrible. Young froghoppers make a ball of frothy "cuckoo spit" to cover themselves up as they suck plant juices.

*Froghoppers can hop well, like frogs.*

*The froghopper's pattern is like the ladybug's, which has black spots on a red body.*

## Shields and stinks

Shield bugs have a hard, shield-shaped covering over the thorax. Some "shields" are green for camouflage, but the orange shield bug's bright colors make it easy to see as it feeds among the leaves. When in danger, it oozes a stinking liquid.

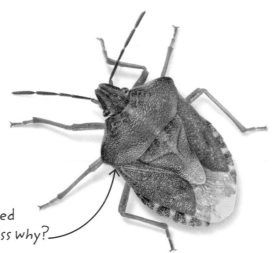

Shield bugs are also called stinkbugs—can you guess why?

The hoverfly does not have a sting at its rear end.

## Pretending to be dangerous

Some insects have warning colors, like this hoverfly, yet they are not harmful. They copy the patterns of harmful insects, such as wasps. Predators who learn to leave wasps alone do the same with hoverflies. This "copying" is known as mimicry.

## Black and yellow

Yellow and black stripes are common warning colours in the animal world. In wasps and bees they advertise their danger to sting other animals.

⚠ The wasp looks like the harmless hoverfly, but has a sting.

# A good cover-up

Some insects look like insects. Others don't. They look like bright green leaves, old brown leaves, colorful petals, twigs, buds, thorns, or even bird droppings. Such a disguise helps the insect to stay unnoticed by predators. Some insects frighten off predators with marks like huge, fierce "eyes."

## Prickly problem

Thornbugs suck the sap of plants such as roses and brambles. Their bodies are shaped like the plant's own thorns and prickles, which few predators want to eat!

Eyespots look like those on a peacock's tail. This is why it's called the peacock butterfly.

Thornbugs have to stay still for their disguise to work.

## Butterfly or hawk?

With wings folded over its back, in its resting position, the peacock butterfly looks like a piece of bark. But when in danger, it opens its wings and flashes huge eyespots, pretending to be a hawk.

The dark markings on the underside of the wings help it to blend in with the bark.

Thorns are like the insect's spines.

Claws on the feet grip the twig securely, even in a strong wind.

The flattened bulges on the legs look like the blades of old, shrunken leaves.

## Spiny stick

This giant spiny stick insect, up to 8 in (20 cm) long, blends in perfectly with the prickles and curly leaves on which it's perched, so predators ignore it.

The bent abdomen has spiny edges, like the leaves and twigs around it.

## Crab spider

The crab spider hunts insects that visit flowers. It sits on petals, waiting to ambush its prey. Depending on the color of the flower on which it is sitting, the spider changes its color.

## Cricket camouflage

The bright color of the green bush cricket is like the green leaf it sits on. Blending in with the surroundings like this is called camouflage.

# Living in the yard

Even the neatest, best kept park or yard is home to thousands of insects. In the summer you can see them crawling in the soil, climbing up plants, eating leaves, and buzzing or flitting from flower to flower. If it gets cold, they hide in cracks in walls or under roofs.

### Careful mother

In springtime, earwigs lay their pearly, oval-shaped eggs. The mother earwig is one of the few insects that cares for her eggs. She licks them all over, to keep them from getting moldy.

The beetle defends itself by arching its tail and squirting horrible-smelling liquid from its rear-end.

### Nighttime hunter

You won't see the devil's coach-horse beetle by day, unless you look in damp places under stones, leaves, or logs. It comes out at night to catch tiny caterpillars, worms, and spiders.

Devil's coach-horse beetles can also deliver a painful bite!

# BORROWING INSECTS

To study insects, borrow them from nature using a pitfall trap. You'll need a jam jar, a trowel, four small stones, and a flat stone. Afterward, put them back in the same place. Are the same insects as active by day as by night?

1. In a sheltered corner, dig a small hole in the ground, just big enough for the jam jar. Put some old leaves in the jar. Find four small stones.

2. Put the jam jar in the hole, its rim at ground level. Place the flat stone over it, propped up on the smaller stones, to keep out rain.

3. During the day, look in the jar every two or three hours. Note which insects have fallen in. Remove the jar when you've finished and release the insects.

## Fast weaver

The garden spider has a white cross on its back and can be found building its web in parks and yards. It constructs webs up to 2 ft (0.6 m) in diameter to catch flying insects. Like most orb spiders, this spider also takes only half an hour to spin its web.

# Living in the woodlands

Woodlands are ideal places for insects. The trees provide food and shelter for hundreds of different kinds of insects. Leaves, buds, fruits, and seeds are all food for plant-eating insects. Hunting insects prey on the plant-eaters. Some insects burrow into living wood, or eat molds growing under loose bark. Others feed deep in roots or rotting wood.

*The beetle's huge antlerlike jaws are not strong enough to bite you.*

*It uses its antennae to feel its surroundings.*

## Stag beetle
A stag beetle larva looks like a big, white worm. For three years it lives in an old woodland log or stump, eating the wood. Then it becomes a pupa, and finally an adult. Only males have the huge jaws, which look like deer antlers.

*The stag beetle has wings under its body casing.*

## Living in a leaf

Green-oak roller moths are found wherever oak trees grow. The young moths (caterpillars) roll up oak leaves and eat them by the thousands!

*The caterpillar rolls itself inside an oak leaf to hide from predators.*

*Green-oak roller caterpillar*

*Green-oak roller moth*

## Gall-makers

Some tiny wasps, flies, and other insects live, feed, and lay eggs inside leaves, twigs, and buds. The tree grows a tough wall around the eggs, and seals them off. These growths are called galls. They come in many strange shapes. Look out for lumps on twigs and leaves.

*Oak-apple galls, made by tiny wasp larvae, look like small green apples that slowly turn brown.*

## A dash of color

A peacock spider is commonly found in Australian woodlands. The back of the male spider's abdomen is multicolored. It raises this like a colorful fan to attract the female.

# Living in the desert

Deserts are too dry for most animals. However, many insects can live there, especially beetles. They usually hide by day, to avoid the hot sun. At night, they feed on plants, windblown seeds, or each other. Some burrow into desert plants such as cacti. Others feed on the bodies of creatures that died from heat or thirst.

## Sandy beetle
This desert darkling beetle is sand-colored, to hide it from enemies. Its larvae look like worms or maggots, and they burrow into the sandy soil, like earthworms do in moist ground.

The ant lion larva squirts special juices into its prey, then sucks out its insides.

## Sand trap
The ant lion larva, also called a doodlebug, digs a cone-shaped pit in the desert sand and hides at the bottom. When an ant tumbles in, the larva grabs it and eats it.

## Adult ant lion
Adult ant lions look a bit like lacewings. The males of some kinds dance in midair in swarms to attract females at breeding time.

## Moth and flower

The small yucca moth lays eggs in the flowers of yucca plants, which live in the desert. In doing so, it carries pollen from one yucca plant to another, so the seeds can develop. In return, the yucca moth's caterpillars eat some of the developing seeds.

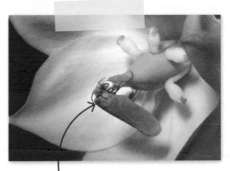

The pollen of the yucca flowers is carried only by the yucca moths.

Long legs for fast scuttling.

## White on white

The white beetle's color serves two purposes. It hides it from predators as it scuttles over the white sands. It also reflects the heat of the sun, allowing the beetle to hunt for longer during the day.

White wing covers protect delicate wings beneath.

The beetle's large legs give a good grip on the soft desert sand.

## Six-eyed sand spider

The six-eyed sand spider often holds sand grains between its body hairs for camouflage. Highly venomous, it buries itself just under the desert surface and ambushes its prey.

# Living in the water

Next time you're passing a pond or river, take a closer look at the water. Many insects make their homes in water. There are insects that skim over the surface, and ones that swim upside down. There are some insects, such as dragonflies, that only live in water when they are young.

The male has a smooth back like this. The female has grooves on her back.

## Dreaded diver

The great diving beetle lives in ponds and has a fierce reputation. With its powerful jaws, it attacks small fish and tadpoles, as well as other beetles. Be careful around them.

The beetle stores air under its wings.

Bristles on legs spread out to make "oars" to row the beetle through the water.

A hard case on the back covers two wings.

Front legs are clawed for helping to grasp prey.

## Young dragonfly

The dragonfly nymph lives in the pond for several years after hatching, before turning into an adult. Be careful—it can bite!

## DIPPING FOR INSECTS

Dip a net onto the bottom of a pond or river, then sit still. When you see an insect, gently lift your net. Turn it inside out in a bucket with water from the pond or river.

⚠ Approach the edge of the water carefully.

The body and tail bristles trap air for the nymph to breathe.

## Baby beetle

The diving beetle nymph either walks along the bottom or swims using its legs as oars. It breathes through a long tube in its tail. This works like a snorkel to take in air at the water's surface.

Like its parent (opposite), the nymph is a ferocious hunter.

Huge, sharp mouthparts spear tadpoles, small frogs, and fish. Mind your fingers.

## Upside-down bug

This kind of water boatman rows just underneath the surface of the water, using its bristle-covered legs. It has a sharp bite, so be careful of your hands and fingers.

# Living in the tropics

Millions of different kinds of insects live in tropical forests. Insects love the warmth and dampness. There are plenty of plants to feed on and hide in and masses of tiny animals to catch. You may often see the largest, strangest, and most colorful insects in these places.

## All that glitters

The mirror spider is found in Australia. The silvery spots on the abdomen reflect light. This provides good camouflage, as the spider looks like raindrops in its rain-forest home.

*Long legs and claws grip the edges of the leaves.*

## Leaping beetle

The back legs of the frog beetle are long and strong, like a frog's legs. It uses them to cling onto vegetation.

*The rear pair of legs fold back on themselves.*

## AS BIG AS YOUR HAND

Hold out your hand and measure 6 in (15 cm) across. This is the size of the goliath beetle from tropical Africa. Now hold a medium-sized apple. This is about how much it weighs.

Goliath beetle

Eyespot

## A sudden fright

The lantern bug usually has its wings folded. But when danger threatens, it quickly spreads its wings to flash two huge false "eyes." They look like the eyes of an owl. Their sudden appearance frightens off most attackers.

The pink-flower mantis has thornlike eyes.

## Double disguise

The pink-flower mantis looks like a flower. It is found on orchids. When small creatures come searching for pollen or nectar, it grabs them in its front legs. This disguise also protects the mantis from predators, such as birds and lizards.

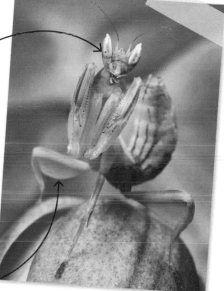

The lobes on the legs look like flower petals.

# Index

# Acknowledgements

Dorling Kindersley
would like to thank:

Helen Peters for the index.
Caroline Stamps for
checking the text.
Anne Damerell for
legal advice.

*The green
rose chafer beetle*

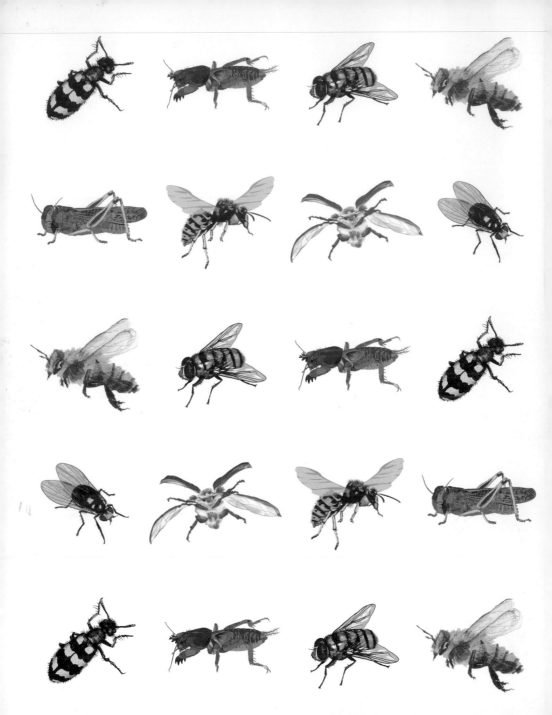